The Two of Us in Each of Us

Journeying to Wholeness

Pastor Emanuel Lambert, Sr.

The Two of Us in Each of Us
Copyright © 2020, 2022 by Emanuel Lambert, Sr.

Published by iGospelShare Ministries
Havertown, Pa 19083

Unless otherwise noted, all scriptures are from the KING JAMES VERSION (KJV): KING JAMES VERSION, public domain.

ISBN: 978-0-9833638-3-5

Cover Design by: Wayne Hill, Sr.

Dedication

This book is dedicated to my wife, for being the wind beneath my wings for 42 years and counting. To my children for believing in me. And to My namesake, in particular, for holding me accountable until I completed this project.

Acknowledgements

I want to thank the Taylor family, Reverend Joy R. Taylor in particular, who worked and wrote with me on this tedious project without complaint. I want to thank her wonderful husband, Deacon Michael Anthony Taylor, for his graciousness and encouragement on this project.

And I, of course, want to thank my god daughter, Sarah Rose Taylor for settling our literary disputes that I would still probably be contemplating over.

And I want to thank Pastor Frederick Scott, Jr. and Dr. Tina Scott for making and helping me to finish this book.

Table of Contents

Foreword

It is known that a proper bibliology, forms a proper theology, which affects our psychology, which gets us a better understanding of our anthropology, which will help us function in our sociology.

This is what has been penned by the capable hands of Pastor Emanuel Lambert Sr. Read it and reap from it and your life will never be the same.

Dr. Keith W. Reed, Sr.
Senior Pastor
Sharon Baptist Church
Philadelphia, Pa

Preface

Have you ever read a book that gripped, grabbed, grappled, and pulled from you and intuitively showed you what God has placed in you and you knew at that moment that you would never get enough learning about the crown creation of God called man, or more accurately the creation known as the human species; which is man and woman.

That is what happened to me in 1983 while a student at Manna Bible Institute when taking a class in Biblical Psychology. The required reading was a book by the title of *Understanding People* and that book watered the seed for me to pursue and try to understand the trichotomy of man and thus this book.

Please know that this book was birthed out of the labor pains culminating and accumulating from the many years of teaching, preaching, counseling and most importantly, intentionally and deliberately attempting to grow while I live.

THE TWO OF US IN EACH OF US
βιβλιος ψυχηλογια

There is a narrative in John Chapter 5 about an ailing and incapacitated man at the pool of Bethesda. It informs us that he had been there for 38 long years "in that case." The good news is that Jesus took note of his case and asked the man a very poignant and interesting question, "Wilt thou be made whole?" The word "whole" is the Greek word "υγιης," which means to become something other than what you are right now, healthy. In other words, Jesus is asking him do you want your life to become progressively better. The man complained and explained why he could not become progressively better. Jesus in his stern, compassionate way, as only He can, abruptly interrupted him, because he saw the solution as more important than the reason. In so many words Jesus said, "Shut up, rise up and take up your bed and walk." The Bible says, "and immediately the man was made whole, and took up his bed and walked."

The reason we should all be so encouraged by this pericope is because it's one that carries with it so much hope. We are taught that regardless of how long we've been in "our case", we can still become progressively better or in Jesus' words, we can be made whole. According to the referenced biblical work, it took place immediately, which suggests it does not take as long to be made whole as one might think when we are in Christ. That is especially encouraging seeing as we all live with the realization that there are two of us in each of us and they are at war one with the other. (Galatians 5:17).

This book will attempt to help Kingdom dwellers in our journey and our struggles in a realistic and comprehensive manner to recognize this truth and to conduct ourselves in accordance. Prayerfully, this book will aide and assist through the power of the Holy Spirit, in our experiencing deliverance from our strong holds, healing of our emotions and the strengthening of our resolve. Prayerfully this book will make us progressively better.

Chapter One

THE COMPLEX NORMALITY OF MANKIND

"What is man, (ανθροπος, a human being) that thou art mindful of him? And the son of man, (ανθροπου, the human race) that thou visitest him? Psalms 8:4

Section One:
The Trichotomy of Man – Genesis 2:7

The sacred sanctified chrestomathy says, "We are fearfully and wonderfully made: marvelous are thy works; and that my soul knoweth right well - Psalm139:14

Man is the crown and most magnificent part of God's creation----far more complex in design and structure than the earth or any heavenly constellation. Consider the design of just one square centimeter from the tip of your baby finger. If you could see them, you would find 1,300 nerve endings. An average square centimeter of skin has twelve feet of nerves and three feet of blood vessels.

Beneath the surface of our skin lies a complex system of muscles, internal organs, nerves, arteries, veins,

9

lymph nodes, joints, and bones; a world of exquisite detail that we all rely on for our health and vitality, but one to which few of us ever give more than a passing thought.

The human body, the crowning glory of God's creation; is superior and superlative to anything that modern technology can build. The bones for example; are more efficient than any building material any engineer can design. One cubit inch of bone scientist say can withstand two tons of pressure, and unlike any other building material, living bone can lubricate and repair itself.

The intricate sophisticated Jehovistic workings of the human body points to God's unfathomable inexplicable wisdom in creation and causes us to emote, erupt and exclaim with the Psalmist: "I will praise thee! for I am fearfully and wonderfully made: marvelous are thy works; and that my soul knoweth right well.----Ps.139:14

As miraculous and complex of a creation as humankind is, creating him was all in a day's work for God. On the sixth day, God said, let us make man and thus God made a trichotomous man. He touched and formed him from the dust of the ground and breathed his life in man via his nostrils and man became a living soul.

It is here that I would like to look at an abridged abbreviated explanation concerning the trichotomy of man and woman. Man and woman consist of body, soul and spirit.

BODY

The body consists of five senses which are hearing, seeing, tasting, smelling and touching. This body is what we live in on this side of life and eternity. The body since that fateful day of disobeying the command of God now comes with planned design obsolescence and an expiration date; it's called sickness and death.

SOUL

Then there's the soul in which the <u>intellect</u>, <u>emotions</u> and <u>will</u> is housed. Our what and how we think, our what we feel and our what we do is resultant of our soul. It's that priceless eternal entity that distinguishes us from the animals and enables us to function beyond instinct by allowing us to think, feel and make a choice.

SPIRIT

Lastly, our spirit which is the noblest part of man and is the breath of God that provides us with life and occupies the innermost part of our being consisting of conscience, intuition and communion. It's the aspect of our trichotomy that God communicates with us through.

Conscience is the Greek word συνειδησεως suneideseos which is the psychological faculty in man and woman that distinguishes between right and wrong, i.e. moral sensitivity. It is the inner voice or the voice in one's heart or how one knows right from wrong.[i] It's been referred to as the monitor of God.

Intuition is the Greek word αισθητηριο aistheterio which is perception and esoteric knowledge. It is the ability to understand something immediately, unpremeditated, without the need for people, things, events or conscious reasoning. [ii] As believers many times we are accused of being "spooky" however, we are not being "spooky" we are being intuitively, numinously, anagogically perceptive when we say "We received it in our Spirit", that is intuition.

Communion is the Greek word κοινονια koinonia. It is the part of our trichotomy that died in the garden, when we disobeyed God and ate off of the forbidden fruit. Yet our spirit even in its present state, longs to be associated and in communion with God or someone or something greater than ourselves. If not regenerated, as God prescribes, the communion facet of our spirit will lead us to idolatry and religiosity instead and in place of a relationship with Christ.

The body was created to serve God.

The soul was created with the purpose of the intellect to think about God, with emotions to love God, and with the will to obey God.

The spirit was created for God to communicate with us without external interference by way of our conscience, intuition, and communion.

"Wherefore, as by one man (Adam) sin entered into the world, and so that all have sinned." And as a result of sin things has gone horribly wrong.

Our body is by disposition opposed to serving God and is perpetually in pursuit of passion and pleasures.

Our soul thinks about anything and everything but God.
Our soul loves seemingly anything and everything but God.
Our soul obeys anyone and everyone instead of God.

Our spirit is displaced from God and has replaced Him with the religion of our choosing.

Which unfortunately causes our normality to be a cataclysmic conundrum.

What in its origin, was created to allow us to live in harmony with God, nature and mankind, now causes just the contrary which makes our normality complex.

And though as believers we have an advantage over unbelievers, yet we also have the reality of the contradictions in and of our lives that seemingly defy logic. We are both wise yet foolish, open yet reserved, facile yet obstinate, non-vindictive yet a deep thirst for revenge. That is our complex cataclysmic conundrum. Thus, we are told that "wisdom is the principle thing but in all our getting get understanding;" to paraphrase, if we knew better, we could do better.

As we move and modulate to section two, let's continue our quest to discover the person we many times know the least about. Because usually this is the person we are the most partial towards. If you have not figured it out by now, at the expense of redundancy, this person is usually the person staring back at us when we look in the mirror.

Section Two:
Personality Profile Hypothesis - Psalms 51:4-5

The proverbial writer unequivocally states that "Wisdom is the principle thing; therefore get wisdom: and with all thy getting get understanding." And with that being said, I am convinced that we cannot appropriately and or properly deal with that in which we don't understand. This stands to reason that many go untreated by the only person that can heal us because we refuse to accept and "understand" the truth about us.

David said, not as an excuse but because he understood, "Behold I was shapen in iniquity; and in sin did my mother conceive me."

In the Septuagint the word "behold" is pointing out something that it wants the reader or hearer to give attention to for understanding. David is saying in essence, I'm not excusing nor condoning my sin, however I understand that there are some fractures in my genetic deoxyribonucleic acid that keeps me from hating wrong as I should. And just like David we all come from the womb with this struggle, and I need to emphatically declare right here "that the struggle is real."

We are born anti-law and full of sins; that's why we need to be regenerated. I was shapen in ανομος, which means by definition lawlessness, wickedness, and sin which makes us unmusical, unmelodious, inharmonious, harsh, strident, clashing, hit a wrong or sour note, turmoil or hurt your ears, and gruff.

We are born this way however; the moral and spiritual level of our parents, will determine how long information contrary to our lawless, genetic, philosophical system gets checked and corrected by our parents.

I personally Biblically and scientifically believe, this is due to our individual diagrammatic personality profile which tells us what kind of unmelodious behavior we have a proclivity toward; thus it becomes our responsibility to recognize, realize and revise our behavior so that we can be, more of what we should be. So in chapter two we will begin to take a more extensive look at the various components and moving parts that makes up our particular and specific variegated personalities.

Chapter Two

TEMPERAMENTS

According to Tim Lahaye, noted as a foremost authority on the subject of temperaments, "There is nothing more defining about people than their inherited temperament! It is temperament that provides human beings with the distinguishing qualities that make each of us as individually unique as the differing designs God has given to fingerprints. Temperament is the unseen force underlying human action, a force that can complicate the life of an otherwise normal and productive human being unless it is recognized, disciplined and directed.

Temperament provides both our strengths and weaknesses. Although we like to think only of our strengths, everyone has weaknesses!" [iii] Tim Lahaye further says, "The theory of the four temperaments is not perfect; no theory of human behavior is. The four temperaments were given names by Hippocrates (c.460 – c. 370 BC), said to be the father of modern medicine. Galen, a Greek doctor, came up with a detailed list of the strengths and weaknesses of the four around A.D 200.

This has remained pretty much intact throughout history" and has been proven to be a viable tool for interpreting personality even in our own lives. [iv]

How Temperaments Come About

It is believed temperaments are the combination of inborn traits that subconsciously affects a portion of our behavior. These traits, which are passed on by our DNA, are based on hereditary factors and arranged at the time of conception. Six people contribute through the genetic pool to the makeup of every baby:

two parents and four grandparents. The alignment of temperament traits, though unseen, is just as predictable as the color of eyes, hair, or body type. It is a person's temperament that makes that person outgoing and extrovertish or shy and introvertish. This gives answer to the question why can two people from the same parents be complete, polar opposites?

Take Jacob and Esau, Issac and Rebecca's kids in Genesis chapter 25 – same parents – different temperaments. Jacob was a homebody, had a gentle manner and loved to cook. Esau, on the other hand, was a rough, ruddy, outdoorsman and loved to hunt.

It should be noted, although temperaments affect our character and personality, temperaments differ from character and personality.

Character by definition is the complex of mental and ethical traits marking and often individualizing a person. The Bible refers to character as "the hidden person of the heart" (1 Pet. 3:4). Character simply put is the real you. It is who you are when no one is watching. It is reflected by your choices when you have options. But what makes character so special is that you take part in the developing thereof. I believe God does that on purpose so we will value it when we obtain it because of all the work that goes into it.

The difference between character and temperament is temperament is passive while character is active. Temperament comes from family affiliation; character comes from individual perspiration. However, personality syllabicated explains the difference between temperament, character and personality. The root word "person" means who you are and what you are. The connecting vowel and suffix "ality" means the condition of. So, it stands to reason that your personality is the present condition of your person. Which is good news, because we can always improve the condition of our person.

Temperaments

Now back to the issue at hand. As mentioned earlier, there are four temperaments: **(1)** Sanguine, **(2)** Choleric, **(3)** Melancholic, and **(4)** Phlegmatic.

Sanguine

People with the sanguine temperament tend to be lively, sociable, carefree, talkative, and pleasure seeking. They may be warm hearted and optimistic. However, there are two of us in each of us. Along with this temperament as with them all, comes pros and cons; favorable traits and unfavorable traits. The unfavorable traits of the sanguine[v] are:

1. _Superficiality._ The sanguine person does not penetrate the depth or the essence of things. He does not embrace the whole but is satisfied with the surface shallow understanding and with a part of the whole.

2. _Instability._ Because the impressions made upon a sanguine person do not last, they are easily followed by others. The consequence is a great instability which must be taken into account by anyone who deals with such persons, if he does not wish to be disappointed.

3. _Tendency to the external._ The sanguine does not like to enter into his inner self but directs his attention to the external environment. This leaning to the external is shown in the keen interest which the sanguine pays to his own appearance, as well as to that of others; to a beautiful face, to fine and modern clothes, and to good manners. In the sanguine the five senses are especially active.

4. Optimism. The sanguine looks at everything from the bright side. He is optimistic, overlooks difficulties, and is always sure of success. If he fails, he does not worry about it too long but consoles himself easily creating problems with learning from mistakes.

Choleric

Choleric people are people of enthusiasm; they are not satisfied with the ordinary and crave for great success in all life affairs. The natural virtue of the choleric is ambition; his desire to excel and succeed despises the little and vulgar and aspires to the noble and heroic. [vi] In brief, people of choleric temperament possess multiple strengths:

* Born leader
* Dynamic and active
* Compulsive need for change
* Must correct wrongs
* Strong-willed and decisive
* Unemotional
* Not easily discouraged
* Independent and self sufficient
* Exudes confidence

As with all of the temperaments, strengths are coming hand-in-hand with *particular weaknesses*. For example, independence and self-sufficiency can easily segue and parlay into pride, anger, and lack of compassion which are considered the main traits of the choleric personality and may show themselves in multiple instances:

1. *The choleric is full of himself.* He has a great opinion of his good qualities and his successful work and considers himself as something extraordinary and as one called upon to perform great feats. He considers even his very defects as being justified, nay, as something great and worthy of praise; for instance, his pride, his obstinacy, his anger.

2. *The choleric is very stubborn and opinionated.* He thinks he is always right, wants to have the last word, tolerates no contradiction, and is never willing to give in.

3. *The choleric has a great deal of self-confidence.* He relies too much upon his own knowledge and ability. He refuses the help of others and prefers to work alone, partly because he does not like to ask for help, partly because he believes that he is himself more capable than others and is sure to succeed without the help of others.

4. *The choleric is domineering and inordinately ambitious.* He wants to hold the first place, to be admired by others, to subject others to himself. He belittles, combats, even persecutes by unfair means those who dare to oppose his ambition.

Melancholic

Melancholic people are deep thinkers, reserved, analytical, usually talented and creative as well as artistic and musical. Their strengths also include being faithful and devoted friends, aesthetically cognizant, sensitive, organized, and neat. Other strengths that accompany the melancholic temperament consist of: [vii]

*Great Teachers

*Encourages Others

*Controlled self-discipline

*Empathetic to others

*Believes in the letter of the law

*Perfectionist

*Self-Sacrificing

*Trustworthy

* Self Motivated

But on the other hand, as with the other temperaments, there are other aspects to the melancholic temperament.
Weaknesses:

1. *The melancholic is moody and prone to depression.*
The person with this temperament has the proclivity to be a

candidate for manic depression. They have an acclivity to not forgive easily. They enjoy being hurt and have a tendency to be victims and martyrs. In addition, the person with the melancholic temperament is critical of self and others.

2. *The melancholic is pessimistic.* They seemingly always remember the negative. The person with the melancholic temperament has a predisposition to linger on past hurts and seems to enjoy it. They brood over things, are absorbed by their thoughts, and are hard to get along with.

3. *The melancholic is very suspicious.* They are too introspective, they set very high, hard standards, they are hard to please, it is hard to meet up to their standards and can be resentful when not appreciated.

4. *The melancholic can be a hypochondriac.* They can be of selective hearing, very proud, impractical, self-centered, and slow to make a decision. People with this particular temperament are exasperated by disorder.

Phlegmatic

Phlegmatics are generally calm and unemotional, self-content, and kind. They are very consistent, relaxed, rational, curious, and observant, making them good administrators and diplomats. Like the sanguine personality, the phlegmatic has many friends, however the phlegmatic is more reliable and compassionate, typically making the phlegmatic a more dependable friend. Known as the fluid and flowing temperament.[viii]

Notwithstanding, keeping with our theme, as you should know by now, there is always two of us in each of us. The phlegmatic is no exception.

Weaknesses:

1. *Though shy*, this aspect of their personality can inhibit enthusiasm in others. They are very much inclined to ease, to eating and to drinking. They are lazy and are known to neglect their responsibilities.

2. *The phlegmatic person generally has no ambition.* Lofty ideals and goals hold very little appeal to people with this temperament. Even in their faith and piety, comfort may trump penance and self-sacrifice.

3. *This personality temperament has the tendency to taunt and tease.* It can also be stubborn and indecisive. Phlegmatic people typically do not show interest in events, happenings or people around them which if not checked by the phlegmatic can lead to egotism and self-centeredness.

4. *Phlegmatics are resistant to change.* Their tendency to apathy makes change very difficult. They can lack the energy necessary to take advantage of their abilities. Conflict terrifies them. When forced into an argument, they get very upset and distressed, seeking escape rather than victory. If confronted, they are likely to admit that they are in the wrong in order to prevent hostilities.

Do remember as we leave chapter two and enter chapter three, temperaments are not passing moods, or phases in our attitudes. They are the foundation of our emotional natures (i.e. individual temperaments influence specific emotions. Emotions tell us what feelings to respond) which stay constant throughout life, from birth until death, even though every other aspect of our personality may change. Let us keep in mind, temperaments are only one of many facets of a person's personality![ix]

Chapter Three

PDP: PERSONALITY DISORDER PREDISPOSITION

As we continue our exploration and explanation of the miraculous complex normality of mankind, we will now take a look at what we have chosen to refer to as the Personality Disorder Predisposition or better yet, the acronymically "PDP."

I personally do not believe we all have a personality disorder, but I do believe we all have disorder in our personality. To further explain this belief, I again reference Psalms 51:5. Each and every one of us exits our mother's womb raising a ruckus and we never stop. Ruckus is raised by disorder in our personality. It would behoove us to locate the disorder in our personality that raises that ruckus. The Diagnostic and Statistical Manual for Mental Disorders (DSM) gives us at least eleven to choose from.

Personality Disorders:

1. Paranoid Personality
2. Schizoid Personality
3. Schizotypal Personality
4. Antisocial Personality
5. Borderline Personality
6. Histrionic Personality
7. Narcissistic Personality
8. Avoidant Personality
9. Dependent Personality
10. Obsessive-Compulsive Personality
11. Sadistic Personality

Let me note my disclaimer here: The predisposed disorder in your personality can reach far beyond the claims stated in this opus and can be legitimately clinical which may require professional diagnosis and prognosis. Disorder in our personality is not new revelation but greater illumination.

Even people in the Bible displayed disorder in their personality, they just did not have names for them. I am persuaded and thoroughly convinced if we are going to effectively live above and beyond the disorder in our personality, we've got to be able to call it by name. Our example, Jesus the Christ in the Book of Mark 8: 9-13 asked the demoniac his name. It's just something that gives you power when you know what you are working with. It's difficult if not impossible to fix what you cannot name. It's hard to fix a "whatchamacallit" because nobody knows what a "whatchamacallit" is, and we usually hide behind our "whatchamacallit."

That is why Adam was commanded by God to name the animals Gen.2:19; so we know just what to call them. Hence, the DSM makes the disorder in our personality distinguishable so we will know how to respond and how not to respond.

God has so fearfully and wonderfully made us that we know us when we hear us. Hopefully and prayerfully and honestly, we recognize our PDP as we come face to face with the other us in us. However, I must insert a caveat, very few of us find anything wrong with the disorder in our personality because to many of us it has become our "normal". What makes it disorder and disorderly is when we want others to see and treat our abnormalities as if they are normal. So, let us grit our teeth and prepare our hearts and further learn about the two of us in each of us.

Let us begin with the compiled Bible characters that I believe represents these personality disorders:

1. **Paranoid Personality**

   Character: Herod the King - Matt.2:1-11,13

   A pattern of distrust and suspiciousness that others' motives are interpreted as malevolent.

2. **Schizoid Personality**

   Character: Elijah - 1Kings.19:9

   A pattern of detachment from social relationships and restricted range of emotional expression.

3. Schizotypal Personality

Character: Witch of Endora - 1Samuel 28:7-11

A pattern of acute discomfort in close relationships, cognitive perceptual distortions, and eccentricities of behavior.

4. Antisocial Personality

Character: Barabbas - John.18:40; Mark.15:7

A pattern of disregard for, and violation of, the rights of others.

5. Borderline Personality

Character: Gadarene demoniac – Luke 8:26-39

A pattern of instability in interpersonal relationships, self-image, and affects, and marked impulsivity.

6. Histrionic Personality

Character: Herodias Daughter, Salome - Matthew 14:6-7

A pattern of excessive emotionality and attention seeking.

7. Narcissistic Personality

Character: Saul - 1Samual 18:5-8

A pattern of grandiosity, need for admiration, and lack of empathy.

8. Avoidant Personality

Character: Timothy – 2 Timothy 1:7

A pattern of social inhibition, feelings of inadequacies, and hypersensitivity to negative evaluation.

9. Dependent Personality

Character: Woman at the well – John 4

A pattern of submissive and clinging behavior related to an excessive need to be taken care of.

10. Obsessive Compulsive Personality

Character: Martha – Luke10:39-42

A pattern of preoccupation with orderliness, perfectionism, and control.

11. Sadistic Personality

Character: The soldiers at the cross - Matt.27:27-31

The sadistic uses aggression to secure dominance and is concerned that others be intimidated and know that it is the sadistic that is the source of their suffering. Their joy is that others know that they are controlled and finally resign themselves to a position of weakness and the sadistic gets pleasure that the person knows it is because of them they have submitted.

Chapter Four

IN A MULTITUDE OF COUNSEL

Because no man is an island we will attempt to further impress our point as it pertains to better identify the disorder in our own personality with help from the medical profession. The DSM defines the general diagnostic criteria for a personality disorder as follows:

A. *An enduring pattern of inner experience and behavior that deviates markedly from the expectations of the individual's culture. This pattern is manifested in (two or more) of the following areas:*
> 1. *Cognition (i.e. ways of perceiving and interpreting self, other people and events).*
> 2. *Affectivity (i.e., the range, intensity, lability, and appropriateness of emotional response*
> 3. *Interpersonal functioning*
> 4. *Impulse control*

B. *The enduring pattern is flexible and pervasive across a broad range of personal and social situations.*

C. *The enduring pattern leads to clinically significant distress or impairment in social, occupational, or other areas of functioning.*

D. *The pattern is stable and of long duration and its onset can be traced back at least to adolescence or early adulthood.*

E. The enduring pattern is not better accounted for as a manifestation or consequence of another mental disorder.

F. The enduring pattern is not due to the direct physiological effects of a substance (i.e., drug of abuse, a medication) or a general medical condition (e.g. head trauma).

Holding fast to the Latin adage, aphorism and axiom that repetition is the mother of memory and learning, I again reiterate though we are not all clinically personality disordered, we all have certain disorder in our personality. These are the descriptions of the various disorders according to the DSM IV:

The Paranoid Personality Disorder

Individuals with Paranoid Personality Disorder are generally difficult to get along with and often have problems with close relationships. Their excessive suspiciousness and hostility may be expressed in over argumentativeness, in recurrent complaining, or quiet apparently hostile aloofness.

Is marked by a pervasive distrust and suspiciousness of others such that their motives are interpreted as malevolent, beginning by early adulthood and present in a variety of contexts, as indicated by four or more of the following:

1. suspects, without sufficient basis, that others are exploiting, harming, of deceiving him or her.
2. is preoccupied with unjustified doubts about the loyalty or trustworthiness of friends or associates
3. is reluctant to confide in others because of unwarranted fear that the information will be used maliciously against him or her
4. reads hidden demeaning or threatening meanings into benign remarks or events
5. persistently bears grudges, i.e., is unforgiving of insults, injuries, or slights
6. perceives attacks on his or her character or reputation that are not apparent to others and is quick to react angrily or to counterattack
7. has recurrent suspicions, without justification, regarding fidelity of spouse etc.

The Schizoid Personality Disorder

The essential feature of Schizoid Disorder is a pervasive pattern of detachment from social relationships and a restricted range of expression of emotions in interpersonal settings.

1. The Schizoid is the Personality Disorder that lacks a personality. Schizoids prefer isolation, as relationships hold no reward for them. They are often described as detached and emotionally flat.
2. neither nor enjoys close relationships, including being part of a family
3. almost always chooses solitary activities
4. has little, if any interest in having sexual experiences with another person
5. takes pleasure in few, if any, activities
6. lacks close friends or confidants other than first degree relatives
7. appears indifferent to the praise or criticism of others
8. shows emotional coldness, detachment, or flattened affectivity

The Schizotypal Personality Disorder

Schizotypals for the most part are known to be odd, eccentric, and socially detached and have serious interpersonal skill deficits. They also have odd thinking patterns; perceptual distortions and their behavior is often considered as weird by others. If religious, they may be drawn to the most extreme and bizarre beliefs and practices.

A pervasive pattern of social and interpersonal deficits marked by acute discomfort with, and reduced capacity for, close relationships as well as by cognitive or perceptual distortions and eccentricities of behavior

1. Can be anagogic, superstitious, and ethereal.
2. odd beliefs and /or magical thinking that influences behavior and is inconsistent with sub cultural norms (e.g. belief in clairvoyance, telepathy, or sixth sense; in children and adolescents, bizarre fantasies or preoccupations
3. unusual perceptual experiences, including bodily illusions
4. odd thinking and speech (e.g., vague, circumstantial, metaphorical, overelaborate, or stereotyped
5. suspiciousness or paranoid ideation
6. inappropriate or constricted affect
7. behavior or appearance that is odd, eccentric or peculiar
8. lack of close friends or confidants other than first degree relatives
9. excessive social anxiety that does not diminish with familiarity and tends to be associated with paranoid fears rather than negative judgements about self.

The Anti-Social Personality Disorder

Interpersonally irresponsible e.g. Is untrustworthy and unreliable, failing to meet or intentionally negating personal obligations of a marital, parental, employment, or financial nature; actively intrudes on and violates the rights of others, as well as transgresses established social codes through deceitful or illegal behavior. The essential feature of Antisocial Personality Disorder is a pervasive pattern of disregard for, and violation of the rights of others.

A. There is a pervasive pattern of disregard for and violation of the rights of others usually seen around the age of 15 years, as indicated by three or more of the following:

1. failure to conform to social norms with respect to lawful behaviors as indicated by repeatedly acts that are grounds for arrest

2. deceitful news, as indicated by repeated lying, use of aliases, or conning others for personal profit or pleasure

3. impulsivity or failure to plan ahead

4. irritability and aggressiveness, as indicated by repeated physical fights or assaults

5. reckless disregard for safety of self or others

6. consistent irresponsibility, as indicated by repeated failure to sustain consistent work behavior or honor financial obligations

7. lack of remorse, as indicated by being indifferent to or rationalizing having hurt, or mistreated, or stolen from another

Borderline Personality Disorder

Unpredictable, manipulative, unstable, frantical fears of abandonment and isolation. Experiences rapidly fluctuating moods. Shift rapidly between loving and hating. Sees self and others alternately as all good or all bad and subsequently will treat you thusly.

A. A pervasive pattern of instability of interpersonal relationships, self-image, and marked impulsivity beginning by early adulthood and present in a variety of contexts. Frantic efforts to avoid real or imagined abandonment. a pattern of unstable and intense interpersonal relationships characterized by alternating between extremes of idealization and devaluation

1. identity disturbance: markedly and persistently unstable self-image or sense of self

2. impulsivity in at least two areas that are potentially self-damaging (e.g. spending, sex, substance abuse, reckless driving, binge eating)

3. recurrent suicidal behavior, gestures or threats, or self-mutilating behavior

4. affective instability due to a marked reactivity of mood (e.g. intense episodic dysphoria, irritability, or anxiety

usually lasting a few hours and only rarely more than a few days

5. chronic feelings of emptiness
6. inappropriate intense anger or difficulty controlling anger (e.g. frequent displays of temper, constant anger, recurrent physical fights)
7. transient, stress related paranoid ideation or severe dissociative symptoms

Histrionic Personality Disorder

Is a pattern of excessive emotionality and attention seeking behavior. Individuals with histrionic personality disorder are uncomfortable and often become depressed and upset when they are not the center of attention

A. Given their drama and theatrics, the histrionic is one of the most reliably identified personality disorders. Described as overreactive, volatile, and engaging, as well as intolerant of inactivity, resulting in impulsive, highly emotional, and theatrical responsiveness; describes penchant for momentary excitements, fleeting adventures, and short-sighted hedonism.

1. as mentioned earlier, is uncomfortable in situations in which he or she is not the center of attention
2. Interactions with others is often characterized by inappropriate sexually seductive or provocative behavior

3. displays rapidly shifting and shallow expression of emotions
4. consistently use physical appearance to draw attention to self
5. has a style of speech that is excessively impressionistic (indirect, suggestive) and lacking in detail.
6. shows self-dramatization, theatricality, and exaggerated expression of emotion
7. is suggestible, i.e. easily influenced by others or circumstances
8. considers relationships to be more intimate than they really are

Narcissistic Personality Disorder

A pervasive pattern of grandiosity (in fantasy or behavior), need for admiration, and lack of empathy, beginning by early adulthood and present in a variety of contexts. Individuals with this disorder have a grandiose sense of self importance

A. Individuals with this personality believe that they are superior, special, or unique and expect others to recognize them as such.

1. Has a grandiose sense of self-importance (e.g., exaggerates achievements and talents, expects to be recognized as superior without commensurate

achievements).

2. Is preoccupied with fantasies of unlimited success, power, brilliance, beauty, or ideal love.

3. Believes that he or she is "special" and unique and can only be understood by, or should associate with, other special or high-status people (or institutions).

4. Requires excessive admiration.

5. Has a sense of entitlement (i.e., unreasonable expectations of especially favorable treatment or automatic compliance with his or her expectations). interpersonally exploitative (i.e., takes advantage of others to achieve his or her own ends).

6. Lacks empathy; is unwilling to recognize or identify with the feelings and needs of others.

7. Is often envious of others and believes that others are envious of him or her.

8. Shows arrogant, haughty, orgulous behaviors or attitudes.

Avoidant Personality Disorder (pg. 672 to 673)

A pervasive pattern of social inhibition, feelings of inadequacy, and hypersensitivity to negative evaluation. These individuals believe themselves to be socially inept, personally unappealing or inferior to others. They're usually reluctant to take personal risk or to engage in any new activities because these may prove embarrassing.

A. Individuals with this disorder will not join in group activities unless there are repeated and generous offers of support and nurturance.

1. Avoids occupational activities that involve significant interpersonal contact because of fears of criticism, disapproval, or rejection.

2. Is unwilling to get involved with people unless certain of being liked.

3. Shows restraint within intimate relationships because of the fear of being shamed or ridiculed.

4. Is preoccupied with being criticized or rejected in social situations.

5. Is inhibited in new interpersonal situations because of feelings of inadequacy.

Dependent Personality Disorder (pg. 675 - 676)

A pervasive and excessive need to be taken care of that leads to submissive and clinging behavior and fears of separation.

A. Individuals with dependent personality disorder may go to excessive lengths to obtain nurturance and support from others, even to the point of volunteering for unpleasant tasks if such behavior will bring the care they need.

1. Has difficulty making everyday decisions without an excessive amount of advice and reassurance from others.
2. Needs others to assume responsibility for most major areas of his or her life.
3. Has difficulty expressing disagreement with others because of fear of loss or support or approval. (Note: Do not include realistic fears of retribution.)
4. Has difficulty initiating projects or doing things on his or her own (because of a lack of self-confidence in judgment or abilities rather than a lack of motivation or energy).
5. Feels uncomfortable or helpless when alone because of exaggerated fears of being unable to care for himself or herself.
6. Urgently seeks another relationship as a source of care and support when a close relationship ends.
7. Is unrealistically preoccupied with fears of being left to take care of himself or herself.

Obsessive-Compulsive Personality Disorder (pg. 678-680)

A pervasive pattern of preoccupation with orderliness, perfectionism, and mental and interpersonal control, at the expense of flexibility, openness, and efficiency.

A. Individuals with obsessive-compulsive personality disorder are reluctant to delegate tasks or to work with others. They stubbornly and unreasonably insist that everything be done their way.

1. Is preoccupied with details, rules, lists, order, organization, or schedules to the extent that the major point of the activity is lost.

2. Shows perfectionism that interferes with task completion (e.g., is unable to complete a project because his or her own overly strict standards are not met).

3. Is excessively devoted to work and productivity to the exclusion of leisure activities and friendships (not accounted for by obvious economic necessity).

4. Is overconscientious, scrupulous, and inflexible about matters of morality, ethics, or values (not accounted for by cultural or religious identification).

5. Is unable to discard worn-out or worthless objects even when they have no sentimental value.

6. Adopts a miserly spending style toward both self and others; money is viewed as something to be hoarded for future catastrophes.

7. Shows rigidity and stubbornness.

Sadistic Personality Disorder (pgs. 513,521)

Only when the inflicting of psychological or physical becomes the organizing principle for the life does an individual become a sadistic personality. Intentionality is thus the core to the definition of the construct.

A. A pervasive pattern of cruel, demeaning, and aggressive behavior. This personality sees kindness as a weakness, it's something about making someone else feel "bad" powerless and ashamed that gives this personality a perverse satisfaction.

1. Has used physical cruelty or violence for the purpose of establishing dominance in a relationship (not merely to achieve some non-interpersonal goal, such as striking someone in order to take something from him or her)

2. Humiliates or demeans people in the presence of others

3. Has treated or disciplined someone under his or her control unusually harshly, e.g., a child, student, prisoner, or patient

4. Is amused by, or takes pleasure in, the psychological or physical suffering of others (including animals)

5. Has lied for the purpose of harming or inflicting pain on others (not merely to achieve some other goal)

6. Gets other people to do what he or she wants by frightening them (through intimidation or even terror)

7. Restricts the autonomy of people with whom he or she has a close relationship, e.g., will not let spouse leave the house unaccompanied or permit teen age daughter to attend social functions
8. Is fascinated by violence, weapons, martial arts, injury, or torture

As stated in the beginning of the chapter, I do not believe we all have personality disorders. However, I cannot state enough that we all do have a proclivity, declivity, propensity and acclivity to a particular personality disorder that strongly influences our behavior which reaches across the aisle of the saved and unsaved; regenerated and unregenerated; with Jesus and without Jesus – born again and not.

Chapter Five

GGG

This is not cyber slang, internet shorthand or netspeak – such as LOL (Laugh out loud), BRB (Be right back), BTW (By the way), FYI (For your information), AAMOF (As a matter of fact), TTYL (Talk to you later) or TGIF (Thank God It's Friday). You get my point. What this acronym stands for is God's Given Gifts.

In explaining these God Given Gifts we are going to use orthodoxy and orthopraxy. Romans 12:4-6 states clearly, "For as we have many members in one body, and all members have not the same office: So we, being many, are one body in Christ, and every one members one of another. Having then gifts differing according to the grace that is given to us, whether prophecy, let us prophesy according to the proportion of faith" That is the orthodoxy.

Notwithstanding, we are born with intuitive gifts from God that enables us to innately do particulars that only require of us to cultivate and improve upon. That is orthopraxy. Intuition resides in the spirit. And it is through the Spirit that God communes with us. God has laden our spirit with gifts from Him. That is why we are able to do things that we discover we can do. They are so innate and unconditional we do not have to be taught to do them. They come what we call "naturally" when in actuality they are not natural, they are supernatural. They are God's Given Gifts (James 1:17).

For example, singing – either you can sing, or you can't. Drawing –either you can, or you can't. If you can't you can doodle at best. The fact that I am gifted in my God given gift enables me to teach you my gift with limitations.

Because the bible says, "God hath dealt to every man the measure etc. (Romans 12:3)" The gifts are so a part of us until all we have to do is uncover, discover, locate, maintain and improve upon them.

For the purposes of this opus, we are using Romans 12: 4-8 to describe the GGG, God's Given Gifts.

4 For as we have many members in one body, and all members have not the same office: 5 So we, being many, are one body in Christ, and every one members one of another. 6 Having then gifts differing according to the grace that is given to us, whether prophecy, let us prophesy according to the proportion of faith; 7 Or ministry, let us wait on our ministering: or he that teacheth, on teaching; 8 Or he that exhorteth, on exhortation: he that giveth, let him do it with simplicity; he that ruleth, with diligence; he that sheweth mercy, with cheerfulness.

~ Romans 12:4-8 (KJV)

The Gift of Prophecy/Prophet
(Speaking Gift)

Definition:

- The special ability God gives to some to proclaim the Word of God with clarity and to apply it fearlessly with a view to the strengthening, encouragement, and comfort of believers and the convincing of unbelievers.

- The special gift whereby the Spirit empowers certain Christians to interpret and apply God's revelation in a given situation.

- The divine enablement to reveal truth and proclaim it in a timely and relevant manner for understanding, correction, repentance, or edification. There may be immediate or future implications.

People with this Gift:

- Expose sin or deception in others for the purpose of reconciliation

- Speak a timely word from God causing conviction, repentance, and edification

- See truth that others often fail to see and challenge them to respond

- Warn of God's immediate or future judgment if there is no repentance

- Understand God's heart and mind through experiences he takes them through

The Gift of Ministry/Service
(Service Gift)

<u>Definition:</u>

- διακιονια – Waiting at tables, active service, ministry, done with a willing (voluntary) attitude, specifically refers to Spirit-empowered service guided by faith

- The gift that enables a believer to work gladly behind the scenes in order that God's work is fulfilled.

- The special ability God gives to some to serve the church in a supporting roll or to invest their talents in the life and ministry of other members of the body enabling them to increase their effectiveness.

- The divine enablement to accomplish practical and necessary tasks which free-up, support and meet the need of others

<u>People with this Gift:</u>

- Serve behind the scenes whenever needed to support the gifts and ministries of others (without having to be asked)

- See the tangible and practical things to be done and enjoy doing them

- Sense God's purpose and pleasure in meeting every day responsibilities attach spiritual value to practical service

- Enjoy knowing that they are freeing up others to do what God has called them to do.

- Would rather do a job than find someone else to do it.

The Gift of Teaching/Teacher
(Speaking Gift)

Definition:

- The special ability God gives to some to explain the truths of the Word of God clearly and to apply them effectively so that those taught understand and learn.

- To instruct others in the Bible in a logical and systematic way so as to communicate pertinent information for true understanding and growth.

- The divine enablement to understand, clearly explain, and apply the word of God causing greater Christ-likeness in the lives of listeners.

People with this Gift:

- Communicate Biblical truth that inspires greater obedience to the word

- Challenge listeners simply and practically with the truths of scripture

- Focus on changing lives by helping others understand the Bible better

- Give attention to detail and accuracy

- Prepare through extended times of study and reflection

The Gift of Exhortation/Encouragement
(Speaking Gift)

Definition:

- The special ability God gives to some to help strengthen weak, faltering and fainthearted folk/Christians in such a way that they are motivated to be all God wants them to be.

- The ability to help others reach their full potential by means of encouraging, challenging, comforting and guiding

- The divine enablement to present truth so as to strengthen or urge to action those who are discouraged or wavering in their faith.

- The special ability God gives some to offer comfort, words of encouragement, hope and reassurance to discouraged, weak or troubled Christians in such a way that they are consoled.

People with this Gift:

- Come to the side of those who are weak in spirit to strengthen them

- Challenge or confront others to trust and hope in the promises of God

- Urge others to action by applying Biblical truth

- Offers advice, an outline for a solution, or a program for progress

- Motivates others to grow and it is the divine enablement to present truth so as to strengthen or urge to action those who are discouraged or wavering in their faith.

- Come to the side of those who are discouraged to reassure them and give them hope

- Emphasize God's promises and confidence in His will.

The Gift of Giving
(Serving Gift)

<u>Definition:</u>

- The gift that enables a believer to recognize God's blessings to respond to those blessings by generously, sacrificially, and cheerfully giving of one's resources (time, talent, and treasure) without thought of return

- The divine enablement to contribute money and resources to the work of the Lord with cheerfulness and liberality. People with the gift do not ask, "How much money do I need to give to God?" but "How much money do I need to live on?"

<u>People with this gift:</u>

- Manage their finances and limit their lifestyle in order to give as much of their resources as possible

- Support the work of ministry with sacrificial gifts to advance the Kingdom

- Meet tangible needs that enable spiritual growth to occur

- Provide resources, generously and cheerfully, trusting God for His provision

- May have a special ability to make money so that they may use it to further God's work.

The Gift of Administration
(Serving Gift)

<u>Definition:</u>

- It's the Greek word προιστημι – which means to set or place before, to set over, to be over, to superintend, preside over, to rule, to be a protector or guardian, to give aid, to care for, to give attention to

- The special ability God gives some to steer the body toward the accomplishment of God-given goals and directives by planning, organizing, and supervising others.

- The divine enablement to understand what makes an organization function and the special ability to plan and execute procedures that accomplish the goals of the ministry

<u>People with this gift:</u>

- Develop strategies or plans to reach identified goals

- Assist ministries to become more effective and efficient

- Create order out of organizational chaos

- Manage and coordinate a variety of responsibilities to accomplish a task

- Organize people, tasks or events

The Gift of Mercy/Compassion
(Serving Gift)

Definition:

- To succor the afflicted, to bring help to the wretched, to show mercy

- The special ability whereby the Spirit enables certain Christians to feel exceptional empathy and compassion for those who are suffering (physically, mentally, or emotionally) so as to feel genuine sympathy for their misery, speaking words of compassion, but more so caring for them with acts of love that help alleviate their distress.

- The divine enablement to cheerfully and practically help those who are suffering or are in need to putting compassion into action.

People with this gift:

- Focus upon alleviating the sources of pain or discomfort in suffering people

- Address the needs of the lonely and forgotten

- Express love, grace and dignity to those facing hardships and crisis

- Serve in difficult or unsightly circumstances and do so cheerfully

- Concern themselves with individual or social issues that oppress people

First Corinthians 12:4 teaches us, "There are diversities of gifts, but the same Spirit". That word diversities in the Greek is *diairesis* and it means that gifts are different, distinct and given in various levels of distribution. We can see through both natural and supernatural gifts, that metaphorically, the human race is likened as unto a human body in that we are supposed to work in unity, in harmony, in sync, in compensation – where even when one lacks the other comes up beside to support and help us accomplish our goals and aspirations – both naturally and supernaturally.

Chapter Six

EKG DIAGNOSIS

I know this is a lot of information but as stated in chapter 1, we are fearfully and wonderfully made. We are more complex than the universe and with that being a scientific fact, how dare we think, believe or suppose that we can know ourselves in such a superficial and cursory manner. I think it is safe to imply that in order for us to know God as we should and others as we should, we must know ourselves as we should. We said all of that to say, there is one more component in beginning to know ourselves. Last, but certainly not least or less, we must consider what type of soil we are.

Significance of Soil

Soils are essential for life, in the sense that they provide the medium for growth. In the natural, soils act as a filtration system for surface water, carbon store and maintenance of atmospheric gases. Soils provide plants with essential minerals and nutrients. It is a agricultural fact that no soil equals no sustenance. Famines are driven by soil degradation. Growth does not occur out of bad soil. Anyone who has done even a little gardening recognizes how the quality of the soil can change the outcome of the harvest.

Many people are aware of what soil texture they are dealing with on sight. All soil looks alike from the texture, but all soil is not alike in the structure. Few people consider a soil's structure, though, even though in most soils, the structure is just as important as the texture. Two soils with the same texture can behave very differently depending on their structure. Texture can be deceitful, but growth reveals the structure. Thus, Mark 4:1-8, Jesus uses the agricultural scene as a parable. A parable is a rhetorical figure of speech, setting one thing beside another to form a comparison or illustration. This parable speaks of soils to represent the hearts of men and women. It is ascertained that every heart bar none is represented in these soils. As we know your heart is a very essential part of your person. The quality of your fruit is determined by the heart it emanates from. That being said, as we continue our journey and odyssey to discover the two of us in each of us, let us honestly and earnestly, with the intention to become better, unearth the condition of our heart.

Four Types of Soil:

1.   Type One - Wayside Soil
2.   Type Two – Stony Soil
3.   Type Three – Thorny Soil
4.   Type Four – Good Soil

TYPE ONE

Wayside Soil

> Mark 4:4
> "And it came to pass, as he sowed, some fell by the way side, and the fowls of the air came and devoured it up."

Culturally speaking in that day, the "wayside" is a path going through the field. It was a road for travelers to travel on when going from one place to another. The travel on the soil would pack the soil and make it hard. The wayside heart or hard heart finds its description and definition in the word "wayside". The Greek word for "wayside" is Odos. This word has a two-fold definition. First, it means hard soil and speaks of a pathway or a road, thus it is soil packed down and hard. It is soil that seed and reason cannot penetrate. Secondly, it means a travelled way, a course of conduct, a fixed way and manner of thinking, feeling and deciding. The "wayside" or hard heart displays three distinct characteristics which are relatively self-explanatory. This type of heart is unreasonable, undiscerning and uninterested. People with wayside hearts are so proud and set in their ways, that they are impervious and oblivious to truth in any form. Some may call this being stuck in their ways. Oh how sad!

> Mark 4:15
> "And these are they by the way side, where the word is sown; but when they have heard, Satan cometh immediately, and taketh away the word that was sown in their hearts"

TYPE TWO
Stony Soil

Mark 4:5-6

"And some fell on stony ground, where it had not much earth; and immediately it sprang up, because it had no dept of earth: but when the sun was up, it was scorched; and because it had not root, it withered away.

The stony ground or soil is shallow soil. Agriculturally speaking, "stony ground", the Greek word "Petrodes", is not to be understood as ground full of rocks. Rather, it is a hard, rocky surface, covered with a thin layer of soil. The condition of this soil would foster a quick growth of seed sown on it. But the layer of rock would prohibit the plant from maturing, for it would oppose any root system and it's obtaining of moisture to sustain the plant and encourage its growth. That quick growth is deceitful, for it appears to be good soil when in truth it is bad soil. The deficiency of this soil or type of heart is seen in times of pain, peril and persecution. Hearts can be accurately measured by how we handle difficult and uncomfortable times. This heart is good as long as things are good. As aforementioned, as soon as pain, peril and persecution come, you find out that faithfulness is not that heart's forte.

Mark 14:16

And these are they likewise which are sown on stony ground; who, when they have heard the word, immediately receive it with gladness; and have no root in themselves, and so endure but for a time: afterward, when affliction or persecution ariseth for the word's sake, immediately they are offended.

TYPE THREE
Thorny Soil

> Mark 4:7
> "And some fell among thorns, and the thorns grew up, and choked it, and it yielded no fruit"

Agriculturally speaking, the thorns in thorny soil are in competition for the good seed. It stops the growth of the good seed causing it to not yield good fruit. Thorny is the Greek word *Akanthas*. It refers to something hidden that hinders growth. Growth is stifled, stymied, suffocated and strangled by this type of heart. This heart is duplicitous. It functions according to its options. It is in competition with and open to stuff it should not have. Though it seems satisfied with the truth it hears, it is longing and lusting for other things. This is a heart full and filled with ambivalence. It's a distracted uncommitted heart.

> Mark 4:18-19
> "And these are they which are sown among thorns; such as hear the word, and the cares of this world, and the deceitfulness of riches, and the lusts of other things entering in, choke the word, and it becometh unfruitful."

TYPE FOUR
Good Soil

> Mark 4:8 And other fell on good ground, and did yield fruit that sprang up and increased; and brought forth, some thirty and some sixty, and some an hundred.

The soil in our text is noted as good soil. Good finds it's definition in the Greek word *kalos* which means fine moral character and pertaining to a fine value. It speaks of accurate, correctly and right. It also means important, of high status, better and to benefit. It means emphatic correctness (to do right on purpose). It means to be healthy and well. The way we know it is good soil is because it produces fruit which is synonymous with growth. Failure to understand God's Word can greatly hinder our fruit bearing. To understand, we must "study to show ourselves approved, etc.". The fruit of the Spirit sprouts forth from good soil: love, joy peace, patience, gentleness, goodness, faith, meekness, and self-control. The good soil will produce fruit from the Word of God in its heart. The amount of fruit will vary as is indicated in this pericope, however if it's good soil it will be evidenced by some fruit. It might be thirty, sixty or hundred, but it will be some fruit. We should all endeavor to produce as much fruit as possible. Let us not forget that the hearts of men and women are weighed and measured by how they respond to the truth. The good heart is a choosing heart. It chooses to do the right thing even when it has options to do otherwise. Options always prove what you really want to do because many of us live according to our options. This is not a perfect heart, but it is a trying heart.

> Mark 4:20 And these are they which are sown on good ground; such as hear the word, and receive it, and bring forth fruit, some thirtyfold, some sixty and some an hundred.

One seed was stopped and stolen. One seed was stunted and scorched. One seed was stifled and smothered. The last seed was strong and steadfast. One of the reasons, I believe soil is likend as unto the heart is because though it is responsible for growth, all soil looks alike from the surface. You find out the quality or what kind of soil you are dealing with according to how it responds to good seed. So it is with the heart, you find out the quality of the heart by how it responds to truth. However, God and life know how to turn less than good soil – good, but not without compost. Compost is decayed organic material used as a plant fertilizer that changes the structure of the soil. In other words, it is trash, garbage, manure which is the equivalent to the problems of life. These things are distasteful and force us to change. Compost allows the soil to form channels and spaces so that the water can reach the soils roots, so it is with our hearts if enough trouble (compost) come in our lives we become more susceptible to hear and do the Word (water) of God.

Chapter Seven

Interlude

A RECAPITULATION AND COMPENDIUM OF SALIENT POINTS

As we intermit, break, recess and pause, let us look again at what we've discussed and discovered thus far:

In Chapter 1, section 1, we considered the miraculous complex normality of mankind. Here we learned about the trichotomy of man which is reflective of our trichotomous creator.

In our study we realized man consists of body, soul and spirit.

The body was created to <u>serve</u> God.

The soul was created with the purpose of the intellect to think about God, with emotions to love God, and with the will to <u>obey</u> God.

The spirit was created for God to <u>communicate</u> with us without external interference by way of our conscience, intuition, and communion.

In Chapter 1, section 2, we talked about the "Personality Profile Hypothesis" extracting as our point of reference Psalms 51:4-5. Which causes us to understand that there are some fractures in our genetic deoxyribonucleic acid (D.N.A.) that keeps us from hating wrong as we should. And just like David we all come from the womb with this struggle, and we need to emphatically declare right here "that the struggle is real." We are born anti-law and full of sins; that's why we need to be regenerated.

In Chapter 2, we showed the affect and effect as well as the bearing of temperaments on the two of us in each of us. Temperament is the unseen force underlying human action, a force that can complicate the life of an otherwise normal and productive human being unless it is recognized, disciplined and directed. The four temperaments being choleric, sanguine, melancholic, and phlegmatic.

Temperament	Traits
Sanguine	Lively, sociable, carefree, talkative, pleasure seeking, warm hearted, optimistic
Choleric	* Born leader * Dynamic and active * Compulsive need for change * Must correct wrongs * Strong-willed and decisive * Unemotional * Not easily discouraged * Independent and self sufficient * Exudes confidence
Melancholic	*Great Teachers *Encourages Others * Controlled self-discipline * Empathetic to others * Believes in the letter of the law * Perfectionist *Self-Sacrificing *Trustworthy * Self Motivated
Phlegmatic	Calm, unemotional, self-content, kind, very consistent, relaxed, rational, curious, observant

In Chapters 3 and 4, we discussed the Personality Disorder Predisposition – PDP which speaks of the specific disorder in our personality. We gathered most of our material from the DSM with the disclaimer that we do not suggest this as a medical diagnosis in no way, shape or form.

1. Paranoid Personality
2. Schizoid Personality
3. Schizotypal Personality
4. Antisocial Personality
5. Borderline Personality
6. Histrionic Personality
7. Narcissistic Personality
8. Avoidant Personality
9. Dependent Personality
10. Obsessive-Compulsive Personality
11. Sadistic Personality

In chapter 5 we realized our God Given Gifts or our triple G (GGG). We are born with intuitive gifts from God that enable us to innately do particulars that only require of us to cultivate and improve upon. Intuition resides in the spirit and it is through the Spirit that God communes with us. God has laden our spirit with gifts from Him. That is why we are able to do things that we discover we can do. They are so innate and unconditional we do not have to be taught to do them. They come what we call "naturally."

When in actuality they are not natural, they are supernatural. They are God's Given Gifts.

In Chapter 6, as we studied the parable of the seed, sower, and soil in the book of Mark, we unearthed – no pun intended- the type of heart we have which biblically speaking is represented by soil. We learned through this study that the heart is branded, classified and measured by how we receive and respond to truth. There are four types of soil being: hard soil, stony soil, thorny soil, and of course good soil.

Chapter Eight

NOW WHAT?

At this point, I'm sure you are asking yourself, "I have read all of this data, now what?" I am so glad you asked. In answer to your question, a good place to start is to use this data to find yourself. Let's not use this time to plead ignorant. Let's not say the convenient "I don't know". You know yourself when you hear or read about yourself. That is why when I was comfortable with being who I was and where I was, contrary to being made whole, I made it my business to avoid the truth, I digress. Because the two of us in each of us is who we think we are and who we are indeed.

Step one: Use the information provided to complete the Personal Identification Paradigm located in the chart below:

	Who Are you?										
Temperament		Sanguine	Melancholic	Choleric	Phlegmatic						
Personality Disorder Predisposition		Paranoid	Schizoid	Schizotypal	Antisocial	Borderline	Histrionic	Narcissistic	Avoidant	Obsessive Compulsive	Dependent	Sadistic
God Given Gifts		Prophetic Speaking Gift	Ministry Serving Gift	Teaching Speaking Gift	Exhortation Speaking Gift	Giving Serving Gift	Administration Serving Gift	Compassion Serving Gift				
Soil		Wayside Soil	Stony Soil	Thorny Soil	Good Soil						

Step two: The Proverbs teach us the value of learning through observation versus participation e.g. the ant and the sluggard - Proverbs 6:6. Let us extrapolate and learn from three Biblical examples.

1. Saul of Tarsus

The first life we will look at or observe is Saul of Tarsus, who we know better as the Apostle Paul.

I think it's safe to say the condition of Paul's person or his personal identification paradigm would look like this:

Personality Disorder Predisposition: OCD

Temperament: Choleric

God Given Gifts: Prophetic

Soil: Wayside at one time, but due to Salvific change and compost in his life, it was made Good.

Saul of Tarsus was determined to up root, tear up, kill, destroy and persecute those who were in "the way" i.e. the followers of Christ. That took a hard heart what the bible refers to as wayside soil. His heart was so hard that at Deacon Steven's stoning, he held the coats so that those stoning Steven could achieve full velocity as they hurled stones to guarantee Steven's death.

I believe that a PHD without GOD can make you a smart Devil. Saul of Tarsus was the worst kind of evil because he was smart and devilish. Not that being smart is evil, but when you use your smarts to be evil that is the worst kind of evil. He was intentional, systematic and religious. For Acts Chapter 9 tells us, that he had his evil sanctioned by the high priests of that day. Verse two tells us that he would obtain legal documentation making it lawful for him to persecute and maltreat the followers of Christ and bring them back bound to Jerusalem. He made his evil lawful. He held the same view as the 45th president of the United States, who has implied that things can be wrong, however it's ok as long as it's not illegal. Thus, was Saul of Tarsus's attitude.

There is a passage tucked away in proverbs that says the Fear of the Lord is the beginning of wisdom which means taking Jesus seriously is our first step to wholeness. In Acts Chapter 9:6, We see Paul's movement towards wholeness. He asks the right question when he recognizes who Jesus is, "Lord what would you have me to do?" And the Lord said to him, "Arise and go". Heeding the voice of Jesus, going, Paul was saved, sanctified and used mightily of God. In his going and growing, historians declaim and declare during his 4 missionary journeys Paul started 14 churches, but it is believed that he started even more. The apex of his growth and wholeness was that God used him to write 13 books of the New Testament. Paul's wholeness blesses believers to this day.

At the end of it all, Paul literally eulogized himself. Paul told us what he wanted us to remember about him in 2 Tim 4:7. He says, "I have fought a good fight, I have finished my course, I have kept the faith: Henceforth, there is laid up for me a crown of righteousness, which the Lord, the righteous judge, shall give me at that day: and not to me only , but unto all them that love His appearing. God makes us whole so that we can be a blessing. Not only to ourselves, but everyone that comes into contact with us.

2. Rahab

Then there is Rahab the newly converted harlot. She is a picture of the luxuriousness of the grace of God which enables us to be whole.

I believe the personality or condition of her person would look like this:

Personality Disorder Predisposition: N/A – not enough information
Temperament: Sanguine
God Given Gifts: Serving Gift – Compassion and Administration
Soil: Good Soil (she brought forth fruit that remained)

We have come to know that names during Bible times were prophetic and quite quintessential. Names were selected based on desire, expectation and/or prognostication. For example, Moses whose name means drawn from the water and he was. Samuel whose name means asked of God and he was. Daniel whose name means God is my judge and he was. And so forth and so on. Rahab whose name means storm, arrogant, or spacious, for reasons only known to her parents. That said, why she was named Rahab is unknown to us, however Rahab was her name.

I do not believe God is calling her Rahab the harlot to shame her. I believe the Lord is letting us know what she was so we can celebrate her and know that we do not have to end up the way we start out. And to show us that none of us and or nothing we have done is out of God's redemptive reach. Because God is able to restore and repristinate. The word repristinate means restore to an original state or condition; to make pristine again. She displays the greatness of God's grace and how it even supersedes our self -destructive choices.

Every life has a story, so let's look at Rahab's story. We first meet Rahab in the second chapter of Joshua. Joshua had dispatched, on a recon mission, two spies to Jericho, the land that God had promised to give to the children of Israel. Rahab knowing who the men were and why they were there, hid them according to Joshua 2:4-7. I believe it is safe to say, as we stated earlier, she had just given her life to Jehovah God because the scriptures clearly tell us in verses 9 - 11 that after observing the glory of God through His mighty acts, she was personally convinced that He was the Lord God of the heavens above and God of the earth below. She obviously had a testimony because 1) the spies went to her house believing they could trust her to help them achieve the will of God and 2) the King of Jericho guesses they might be hiding there also. Word gets around when you love the Lord.

As we continue to learn life lessons by following Rahab's journey to wholeness, we see her brokering a deal with the spies to take care of her and her household by delivering them safely to the people of Israel outside of the city during the destruction of Jericho. One of the sure markings of wholeness is understanding the world is bigger than you and your concerns. Wholeness causes you to look out for others as Rahab did. Furthermore, I believe what also attributed to her becoming whole is she did not dwell on poor life choices or try to blame them on something or someone, although I am sure there were exogenous factors. No, Rahab decided to put her past behind her and push on by getting out and staying out. She gave her life to the Lord and changed her associations as Proverbs 13:20 declares that he who walks with wise men shall himself be wise. Rahab shows us that the first step to getting somewhere is to decide you are not going to stay where you are!

In keeping in step with the grace of God, this converted harlot is mentioned three times in the New Testament: Matthew 1:5, James 2:25 and Hebrews 11:33 which makes her one of the great cloud of witnesses. Rahab married a Hebrew named Salmon who was the father of Boaz who was the father of Obed who was the father of Jesse who was the father of King David. She is the great, great, grandmother of King David which puts her in the family tree and lineage of our Lord and Savior Jesus Christ. This is perhaps one of the most beautiful illustrations of the grace of God and what He can do through you if you let Him.

3. King Saul

Now King Saul on the other hand, is an example of what wholeness is not. Unfortunately, King Saul ended up less of what he was than what we met him as which proves to us that life is of such whereby we can't stand still in what we are. Without exception we are either moving forward or we are moving backwards. We are either progressing or regressing. We are either growing or un-growing. We can never neutrally remain where or what we are.

As we pull King Saul's Personal Identification Paradigm file, we have concluded that King Saul was a straight-out Narcissist:

Personality Disorder Predisposition: Clinically Narcissistic
Temperament: Choleric
God Given Gifts: Exhortation (organized an army of thousands that defeated the Philistines)
Soil: Wayside Soil (Hard Heart)

According to the DSM, having more than five characteristics of the Narcissistic personality disorder say's that you are clinically ill, which made King Saul in need of a clinician. According to I Samuel 8:22, the bible says, talking about the children of Israel, "and the Lord said to Samuel, harken unto their voice and make them a King." Saul was the first King of Israel. The circumstances leading to his selection were as follows: he was privately anointed by Samuel at Ramah, he is publicly acclaimed by Samuel at Mizpah, at this stage, Saul was a very humble man. He felt he was unworthy and actually had to be bought out of hiding when the prophet Samuel officially proclaimed and introduced him as King (1 Samuel 10:21). He later raises an army of 330,000 to rescue a surrounded Israelite city called Gabesh-Gileah from a cruel enemy and thus

77

establishes his ability to lead the Kingdom. But King Saul through his narcissistic personality disorder, fueled by pride, was rejected. No man in the Bible, had so many chances given him to make a success of his life as did King Saul. No man so painfully missed the glorious opportunities afforded him like this man. Not only did he miss great opportunities, but he literally and deliberately abused them. His sun arose in triumph but set in tragic defeat. The degringolade of his life is the old familiar story of pride, self-centeredness, egotism and "thinking more highly of himself than he ought to." And as we all know, pride is always faithful to do what pride does. It precedes destruction.

Let's see how King Saul deliberately DID NOT become whole. After all, he was a man anointed and filled with the Spirit of God (1 Sam 11:6). He had everything he needed to be all he needed to be. That is what God does for us. He gives us everything we need to become all that we need to be. Because God is not going to require anything of us that He does not equip us to do. In his early years, King Saul was humble and practiced self-control (1 Samuel 10:22; 10:27; 11:13).

Somewhere between hiding in the stuff and his military victories, pride got in. If we are going to be whole and remain whole, we have to guard our soul against pride. Pride makes us impatient. Pride makes us think we know best. Prides makes us do everybody else's job. Pride caused King Saul to make a sacrifice that God assigned to Samuel the Priest. This act of prideful disobedience restricted his influence (1 Samuel 13:12-14).

After being fired as King, he continued his decline and was guilty of rash vows (1 Samuel 15:11-23). He then became subject to functioning to his base, small characteristics. Now this is what really keeps you and guarantees you to not be whole: functioning from your lower, base characteristics. He became jealous of David and that occupied and preoccupied most of his life. Not being whole, can have you preoccupied for most of your life pursuing the wrong thing. He patronized the superstition he had forbidden. His behavior belied his word. Which made him a contradiction (1 Sam 28:7). Wounded in battle King Saul, ended up taking his own life (1 Sam 31:4) Oh the tragedy of not aiming at wholeness. The tragedy is that you can never be big staying small because big always trips over small, which keeps us from being big and doing big things. Because the Bible says, "it is the little foxes, that destroys the vine" (Song of Solomon 2:15)

The reason he did not get better, is because he did not get better. The reason he would not change, is because he would not change. The reason he did not improve, is because he did not improve. The way not to be made whole, is to not get better when you should; to not change when you should; to not improve, when you should.

Chapter Nine

THE CONCLUSION OF THE MATTER

At the beginning of this book, Jesus asks the question, "Wilt thou be made whole?" That word "whole" is the Greek word "hugies" where we get our word hygiene which means sound, pure, wholesome and uncorrupted. A cognate to "hugies" is the word "auxano" where we get our word auxiliary which means to cause to increase, to cause to grow, to be enlarged. That is what God wants from us. He wants us to be sound, pure, wholesome, uncorrupted, growing, increasing, enlarging – He wants us to be more. Better yet, He wants us to be the most we can be.

There is a passage in 2 Corinthians 13:1 that helps us in our effort to becoming whole. It clearly states, "At the mouth of two or more witnesses every fact shall be established". At the beginning of this book, we see Jesus as our first witness. Jesus told the man at Bethesda's pool side, "In order to be made whole, you need to do what I say". Regardless of how long you have been in your current state. Regardless of who will and will not help you. Regardless of how you feel. The way to wholeness is to do what Jesus says because John 5:9 tells us "And the man was made whole and took up his bed and walked".

Keeping in step with the scriptures, we find a second witness, which is a reliable witness, because she happens to be Jesus' mother. I am talking about Mary. We find her speaking to the servants while in attendance at a wedding in Canaan of Galilee of an unknown couple that ran out of wine mid reception. Mary simply stated to the servants concerning their conundrum, "Whatsoever Jesus saith unto you, do it". So the conclusion of the matter is, if we are going to be made whole, we've got to take the counsel of our two witnesses. They both said the same thing succinctly. When it comes to Jesus and things being made better, "Whatsoever He saith unto you, do it".

"Walk with the King and be a blessing."

The Epilogue

Continuing Our Journeying
to Wholeness

_____

Pastor Emanuel Lambert, Sr.

Chapter Ten

BE THE CAPTAIN OF YOUR OWN EMOTIONS

PROVERBS 4:23

Introduction

In furthering our pursuit of personal growth or as this book states with the overarching objective "journeying to wholeness", I believe it beneficial to add a helpful addendum to the *Two of Us In Each Of Us*. With that being said, I am totally convinced that if we are going to be more than we are and if we're going to be as Jesus offered, to be made whole, we must be more aware and in control of our emotions. If you would indulge me, let us together, regardless of age, ethnicity or gender see how to excuse-less-ly achieve this necessity.

The Quintessential Significance of EQ

Paul, the inspired writer of First Corinthians 9:27, says concerning this area of Emotional Quotient (EQ), "But I keep under my body, and bring it into subjection: less that by any means, when I have preached to others, I myself should be a castaway (disqualified) KJV". Let's note that first he says "but", which lets us know that Paul knows that if he and or we refuse to do what the Bible imperatively commands us to do, we will get something other than the best results. Because one of the cognates for "but" is "moreover" which means we need something that will moreover override our emotions. Too much of our behavior we allow to be determined by how we feel.

I am convinced that EQ (emotional quotient) is more important than IQ (intellectual quotient) because you can have a high IQ and your EQ can keep you from experiencing all that your IQ can grant you. You can literally be smart in your head and fickled, frivolous, and fallacious in your emotions because emotions have no intellect and are subject to shift premised upon the information they are given. Thus, we need to talk about the quintessential significance of emotions. That is why we are commanded by the God who made us and knows us better than we know ourselves, to guard our heart but in colloquial, contemporary vernacular he is saying to control our emotions.

Because the God who created us knows emotions are a sympathetic function tainted and flawed by sin. Which means they operate from the autonomic soulical system which regulates our psychological unconscious actions. They are passively impulsive which means they just "come up" – which means that they are both exogenous and endogenously reactionary. This information on emotions is to be used to consciously and intentionally as well as conscientiously cause, create, and cultivate trichotomous homeostasis which in turn will birth in us and foster a greater level of wholeness and a fuller life from the inside out.

EQ: Emotional Quotient

E.Q. emotional quotient or plainer disclosed, emotional intelligence is a degree or amount of a specified quality or characteristic. Emotions, we must understand, do not have intellect and are subject to vacillate premised upon the information it is given. We need to know that the heart is more powerful than the mind. It is a known fact; the heart convinces and makes a convert of the mind that is why we are admonished not to follow our heart because of what it's filled with [Mk.7:15-23].

As a matter of fact, Proverbs which is one of the wisdom books of the Bible tells us unequivocally to guard our heart and deductively declares to us that it determines the course of our life. Our emotions are referred to as a Sympathetic Function anatomically speaking or the autonomic nervous system which functions to regulate the body's unconscious actions. One of the sympathetic nervous system's primary purposes is to stimulate the body's fight or flight reflex. It is, however, constantly active at a basic level to maintain proper homeostasis and that's why I reiterate, "Above all else, guard your heart for everything you do flows from it." (Prov 4:23, NIV)

In Biblical times, the Roman soldier's breastplate was used to protect the vital organs such as the heart and intestines. In the Hebrew mindset the heart represented the mind and will. The bowels, or intestines, represented emotions and feelings (Col 3:12, KJV). Therefore, I believe it reasonable to conjecture that the breastplate probably represents guarding our mind and emotions (Which is 2/3 of our soul).

Feelings

Daniel Goleman, the author of Emotional Intelligence, defined emotion as "referring to a feeling and its distinctive thoughts, psychological and biological states, and range of propensities to act." Researchers have classified them (emotions) into eight main families: So the question is..."What emotion is what I'm feeling, emanating from?" (συναίσθημα)

Emotions: Family of Eight

1. Anger
2. Sadness
3. Fear
4. Disgust/Pride
5. Shame
6. Enjoyment
7. Surprise
8. Love

1. **Anger**

   <u>Hyponyms:</u> for Anger include fury, hostility, irritability, and annoyance. Anger is a divalent dyad of an emotion in that it is the best and worst emotion we have. Anger bullies and suffocates and supersedes one's senses and other emotions therefore impairing one's judgment showing us and others our other side notwithstanding in the midst of duplicity it is an excellent boundary gauge in that we get angry when our personal boundaries are violated which says we can measure our boundaries by what makes us angry. Proverbs13:10 says, "Only by pride cometh contention but with the well advised is wisdom". Anger stirs our souls and alerts us when our boundaries are violated. We can also gauge the validity and or pride of our anger by boundary measurement. Ephesians 4:26 tell us to "be ye angry and sin not…"

   The grammatical structure of the word "angry" in this verse is (v.pre.pass.imp.2per.plu.), which is a verb in the present tense in the imperative mood, second person, plural number. Which shows by grammatical interpretation there is great utility in anger. Not only that, but anger causes blood to flow to the hand, making it easier to grasp a weapon or strike at a foe; heart rate increases, and a rush of hormonal cocktail consisting of adrenaline and cortisol generates a pulse of energy strong enough for vigorous action. We'll take a deeper dive into this emotion later.

2. **Sadness** στυγναζω,

Mark 10:22 lets us know that the rich young ruler was sad. The grammatical structure of the word "sad" in this verse is (v.act.aor.part.nom.sing.mas.) which is a verb in the active voice; aorist tense; participle, nominative case, singular number, masculine gender. Sadness is defined as expressive of or characterized by sorrow – despondency, dejection, unhappiness, regret, depression, and misery – which is antithesis to cheer, gladness, happiness, and joy. Sadness brings a drop in energy and enthusiasm for life's activities, particularly diversions (amusement) and pleasures, and, as it deepens and approaches depression, sadness slows the body's metabolism which further lessens energy and if left uninterrupted this has a passive voice re-action. Metaphorically speaking sadness is liken unto the sky covered with clouds, to render gloomy, somberness of speech, crestfallen, discouraged grief, self-pity, solipsism, excessive self-absorption over one's unhappiness and troubles, despair, dejection, and loneliness.

The Bible tells us in Ecclesiastes 3 that there is a time and season for everything under the sun. That word "season" means "set time". Sadness is one of those dangerous emotions because if left uninterrupted too long, it can be detrimental even to the point of deep depression or suicide. That is why God combats sadness by telling us to rejoice in the Lord always and He finds it important enough to repeat it by saying and again I say rejoice (Psalm 37: 3-4; Philippians 4:4). God want us to rejoice which means to make one mildly happy and pleasant versus sadness which produces unhappiness and meanness.

3. **Fear**

Hyponyms: Anxiety, Edginess, Nervousness, Fright, Terror, Apprehension. The biological effect of fear is blood goes to the large skeletal muscles, such as in the legs, making it easier to flee and making the face blanche as blood is shunted or diverted away from it creating the feeling that the blood "runs" cold. At the same time the body freezes, if only for a moment, allowing time to gauge whether hiding might be a better reaction. Circuits in the brain's emotional centers trigger a flood of hormones that put the body on general alert, making it edgy and ready for action, and attention fixates on the threat at hand, the better to evaluate what response to make. Hence evaluation of the reaction of fear is closely bound up with the understanding of one's own existence and ability or inability. The nature of the fear that oppresses man and causes him anxiety means that the absence of fear is regarded as an objective worth seeking.

4. **Disgust**

   Hyponyms: Pride, Complaining, Contempt, Scorn, Aversion, Distaste, Revulsion, Hatred.

5. **Shame**

   Hyponyms: Guilt, Remorse, Humiliation, Embarrassment and Chagrin.

6. **Enjoyment**

   Hyponyms: Joy, Relief, Contentment, Delight, Thrill, Euphoria, Ecstasy, Happy, Well-being.

7. **Surprise**

   Hyponyms: Unexpected Good, Undeserved Good, Shock, Amazement, Wonder, Blessing, Delightful Impulsivity, Amuse, Fascinate, Charm, Enchant, Gladden, Please, Brighten, Elate, Make happy, Warm, Improve

   Antonyms: Depression, Disappointment, Melancholy, Misery, Pain, Sorrow, Trouble, Unhappiness.

8. **Love**

   Hyponyms: Acceptance, Trust, Devotion, Adoration, Care, Appreciation, Regard

Emotions: Foundation to Your Soul

Emotions are the autonomic impulse and sympathetic feelings perceived by the five senses that cause emoting which is response and demand. The mind with its thoughts is the power source. Emotions are often the driving force behind motivation and actions - positive or negative.

In the Liddell & Scott Ninth Edition Greek Lexicon emotional quotient is explained to us. The Greek word su-nais-thema (συναίσθημα) is a very interesting word; it means along with, to be aware of "in" oneself, self-consciousness, conscious perception, awareness, joint-perception. The word "thema" means basic rock and or foundation.

Sunaisthema is an awareness or perception of an inward psychological or spiritual fact; it is intuitively perceived knowledge of something in one's inner self. It speaks of emotional consciousness, better yet it is knowledge of specific emotions which enables us to identify specific emotions and conduct ourselves specifically (Jn.8:32).

Sunaisthema is emotional awareness i.e. being aware of what emotion I am feeling and how it is affecting me either negatively or positively. The word sunaisthema is a derivative of the root word su-nais-thano (Συναισθ-ανω).

As you can see, the root word's ending is "ano" which tells us what we are to do with our emotions. The word "ano" means upward, things that are above, a higher place, the top, superior. Which instructs us that we should have a high level of emotional intelligence; we should have an upward; above average level; our emotional intelligence should be at a high place.

When it comes to emotional intelligence we should strive to be at the top. We should work to have a superior level of emotional intelligence. I personally believe, as a black person, that our community does not place enough significance on the importance and teaching of emotional intelligence/EQ. Reason being, in keeping in step with the title of this section, emotions are the foundation (θεμέλιος). That is why we are commanded in Proverbs 4:23 to guard them. Because the Greek word (θεμέλιος) means foundation; the basis or groundwork of anything.

It is the basis for the rest of you, the authority, the heart, the justification, the underpinning, the reinforcement, and the support. What you are emotionally is what you are.

Society measures you by your emotions. Either you are emotionally stable or unstable. That is how important emotions are.

Negative:	Positive:
1). Anger	1). Enjoyment
2). Sadness	2). Surprise
3). Fear	3). Love
4). Disgust	
5). Shame	

We've got to learn to determine our emotions by being knowledgeable of our emotions so that we can determine them, and they don't determine us. That is why the proverbial writer tells us unequivocally to guard our hearts (Proverbs 4:23). We want to affectively and effectively live a life of prosperity, purpose and intentionality from the inside out.

New Help from the Inside

New nature and fruit bearing Gal.5:22-23

NOUNS

Our new nature is where the fruit is borne from, however there is a caveat: each fruit is a noun. Nouns must be exercised and or executed by a verbal host. This means these nouns need our cooperation in order to be experienced and seen.

The Holy Spirit should be the well spring from where this fruit emanates. A spring is a constant feed. Our emotions should now be fed and fueled by new fruit, and they are all positive.

Fruit of the Spirit:

1. <u>Love:</u> regard, benevolence, good will, esteem, appreciation

2. <u>Joy:</u> delight, gladness, source of joy (Nehemiah - 8:10 – The Joy of the Lord is our Strength…)

3. <u>Peace:</u> one, quietness, rest, harmony, accord, welfare, agreement

4. <u>Longsuffering</u> (makro thumos): slow to respond to anger, forbearance, tolerance, passion (anger) constancy, steadfast, perseverance, fortitude, patience, slowness in avenging wrong, stamina, stability

5. Gentleness: description of one's disposition, tenderness, kindness, humanity; antithesis to bad character, opposite of severity or cutting something short or quickly

6. Goodness (Agathōsúnē): beneficent, generous, doing good, however it does not spare sharpness or rebuke to cause good (agathón) in others; it is more than chrēstótēs which is gentleness and kindness, rather it is a mellowing of character; it is character energized, expressing itself in agathón, which is benevolence and active goodness.

7. Faith: persuasion about God and what God wants you to do, Who He is, and What He is able to do (Hebrews 11:6)

8. Meekness: gentleness of attitude and behavior, in contrast with harshness in one's dealings with others; gentleness, meekness, mildness, humility (Matthew 26:53)

9. Temperance: to exercise complete control over one's desires and actions; to control oneself, to exercise self-control; the anchor of emotions (Proverbs 25:28)

Emotional Intelligence

The Word of God shows us the strength of emotions in Proverbs 16:32, "He that is slow to anger is better than the mighty; and he that ruleth his spirit (emotions) than he that taketh a city".

Emotional intelligence or EQ, the measure of which is referred to as EQ, is often compared to our Intelligence Quotient or IQ. But what is the difference you ask? IQ measures a person's reasoning ability while EQ measures how one manages their emotions. I.Q. Has its advantages however E.Q. has even greater advantages.

E.Q measurement according to the experts are as follows:

1. You are self-aware: Being aware of your emotions as they are happening.
2. You have self-control: We need to be able to act and react based on the situation and not on how we are feeling in that moment.
3. You are empathetic: Being aware of the emotions of others and caring while doing unto others as you would have them do unto you. (Matthew 7:12)
4. You effectively manage change: How we adjust to change is a measure of our EQ, the one that is able to see the change and adjust to it.

5. You don't dwell on the past: You don't stay stuck on failure, but you rise from the ashes of that failure a smarter and more confident individual. (Proverbs 24:16)

6. You control your thoughts: How we talk to ourselves is a measure of our emotional intelligence. (I Samuel 30:6)

7. You pay attention: People with High EQ are measured by not allowing distractions to impair their focus.

Emotional Intelligence Produces Wisdom

Proverbs 24:5–6, "It's better to be wise than strong; intelligence outranks muscle any day. Strategic planning is the key to warfare; to win, you need a lot of good counsel" (The Message Bible)

A high I.Q. with a neglected or distorted E.Q. can make you a smart devil or an intelligent monster, I'm reminded of Ted Bundy who with an I.Q. of a 136 a law student, who killed some believe over one hundred women. Then there's Harold Shipman with an I.Q. Of 140 - a doctor, graduated from Leeds University, killed two hundred fifty plus people and committed suicide in prison. Then there's Ted Kaczynki aka the unibomber a higher I.Q. than Einstein (160) with an I.Q. of 167 - a Harvard graduate and a Harvard mathematics professor who carried on a murder spree for seventeen years by mailing bombs to his victims.

Let it be known, I am not suggesting there is anything wrong with a high I.Q. I'm merely attempting to stress the significance of developing all three: Intellectual Quotient (IQ), Emotional Quotient (EQ) and Spiritual Quotient (SQ). Each quotient emanates from a specific aspect of the trichotomous man that makes him complete in his personage.

Trichotomous health: The Bible says in Genesis 1:26, "And God said, Let us (God speaking of His trichotomous self) make man in our image, after our likeness..." We find out through this verse in God creating man that The Spirit gave life, animation and being to the trichotomous man. That is why in the New Testament in Galatians 5:16 it says, "This I say then, Walk in the Spirit, and ye shall not fulfil the lust of the flesh." According to Genesis 2:7, man is a trichotomous creation with his soul inserted between his flesh and his spirit; choosing his behavior contingent upon which entity of his trichotomy he or she listens to, which in turn will determine the outcome of one's life.

For instance, if the soul responds properly to the Spirit albeit the Spirit of God or the spirit of man which is the noblest part of our trichotomy (which is the breath of God) our deeds will be noble even if it's not for a Godward reason...on the other hand if our soul responds to our flesh we will do and get the "works of the flesh which are these..." Galatians 5:19-21.

Proper Order

Created	Genesis 2:7
Function	Spirit, Soul, Body
Being	SQ, IQ, EQ

The body is the instrument that manifests and displays the decision made. The Bible even puts emphasize on the quintessential necessity of spiritual quotient, though our world and culture pretend to act as if it is insignificant. The Bible says this with clarion reverberation:

1. **Proverbs 1:7** The fear of the Lord is the beginning of knowledge: but fools despise wisdom and instruction.
2. **Psalms 119:98** Thou through thy commandments hast made me wiser than mine enemies: for they are ever with me.
3. **Psalms 119:99** I have more understanding than all my teachers: for thy testimonies are my meditation (Understanding is a spiritual faculty).

We are moved spiritually because we are moved by what we believe which is another Spiritual function. Therefore, without exception being creatures regulated by what we believe, I believe it to be an irrefragable reality to say that we all got and continue to get our belief system from somewhere.

As it pertains to understanding, where you get your understanding from, the object or source of knowledge, proves it's validity. A good question to ask when anyone is giving you information that affects your life, you want to ask them the question, "Where did you get that from?".

Proverbs 1:7 says, "The fear of the Lord is the beginning of knowledge...."

Chapter Eleven

THE UTILITY OF ANGER

EPHESIANS 4:26-27

Anger is (if not the best emotion) one of the best emotions God gave us. Reason being is because anger can work largely for you or largely against you. If handled biblically, which is correctly, anger can literally change one's life by putting us in better control of a very destiny determining emotion. Anger is good in that it is a security mechanism, a fence if you would, in that it protects us. It's in place to protect our self-worth; to protect the boundaries put in place; to protect that which is valuable and when those boundaries are violated, we are autonomically alerted by getting angry.

Anger is a Sympathetic Function: By sympathetic it is meant that it is an automatic, autonomic, impulsive, emotional reaction. It is not manufactured per se; it can be provoked or caused (without your permission) by an outside source. The autonomic nervous system functions to regulate the bodies unconscious actions. It stirs, arouses, awakens, and incites one to activity (Pro.10:12). The word "stirs" means to "rouse" or to raise anger. And of course, anger is to be excited with displeasure.

The sympathetic nervous system's primary process is to stimulate the body's fight, flight or freeze machination. It is, however, constantly active at a basic level to maintain proper homeostasis. Thus, we have anger.

What personally intimates to me that anger is good, is its Greek syntactical grammatical structure. The word anger in the pericope of scripture Ephesians 4:26-27 is the Greek word οργιζω which when parsed i.e. surgically, verbally, dissected (v.pre.pass.imp.2per.plu.) is a verb in the present tense; the passive voice, the imperative mood; in the second person; plural number.

This parsing gives us a workable explanation of the utility of anger or better yet how anger works for us rather than against us. The fact that it's a verb tells us it's an action. The present tense tells us that this occurs in actual time (it's going to happen and it's ok. The passive voice says the subject you,me,us receives the action. The imperative mood means it comes with commands attached. Verse 27 says "to be angry, but sin not". The second person says it is addressed to "you". Plural number means it happens to everybody.

So that says to you and me that anger is: 1.) A character protector 2.) A character gauge and 3.) A character developer.

1. **It's a Character Protector:** It's a Character Protector: in that it lets us know when our God given boundaries have been violated. It's an alarm system of sorts. I believe it's given to us to keep our self-worth healthy. Assuring that we do not allow our conscience to be seared (I Tim.4:2). The conscience συνειδησις is the monitor of God. Other words for monitor include check, advisor, guide, supervisor, and watchdog. When your God given conscience is violated, that is when anger erupts.

2. **It's a Character Gauge:** in that our response to anger helps us to measure our level of pride because the Bible so ingeniously shares with us in Proverbs 13:10 that, "Only by pride cometh contention (anger): but with the well advised is wisdom." So, anger, I believe is safe to say is a plumb line, benchmark, yard stick that measures one's pride. Pride is antecedent to anger and anger precedes pride and pride produces contention.

3. **It's a Character Developer:** It's a Character Developer: in that if handled obediently it helps us to develop our person by asking and answering ourselves a few questions because the bible says in James 1:19 (NIV) "My dear brothers and sisters, take note of this: Everyone should be quick to listen, slow to speak and slow to become angry". That said, the first question I should ask myself is:

a) Why am I angry?

b) Is this a valid violation of boundaries or am I thinking more highly of myself than I ought to (Rom.12:3)?

c) If I am, let me homeostatically adjust myself, so that I can respond properly while not committing sin thus giving the devil room to invidiously stultify, destroy, and devour me by my wrong response (I Peter 5:8). Therefore, let me benefit from the learned lesson of my anger (Ephesians 4:27).

Another benefit of anger is it allows us to detect and determine what type of people are in our friend group. Anger sends an alert and alarm advising us if people are: 1.) peace makers, 2.) peace breakers or 3.) peace takers.

This is quintessential to know because "God hath called us to peace" according to I Corinthians 7:15.

1. **Peace makers**: The Amplified Bible Matthew 5:9 is so stated, "Blessed [spiritually calm with life-joy in God's favor] are the makers and maintainers of peace, for they will [express His character] and be called the sons of God. In the King James Version, Matthew 5:9 reads "Blessed are the peacemakers: for they shall be called the children of God". This verse is saying that the markings of the peacemaker are they are for one

μακαριος, which means in the Greek, they are blessed and happy. The reason they are blessed and happy is because they realize how well off and fortunate, they are which causes them to be grateful which gives them an inward peace that bleeds on those in whom they come in contact. Then there is ειρηνοποιός which in the Greek means loving peace. They are pacific: tending to make and or preserve peace, not warlike, peaceable, and mild. They have a mansuetude disposition. They are conciliatory, calm, tranquil, untroubled, amicable, gentle, friendly, at peace, and neutral. These people will be called the Sons of God because they act like their Father.

2. **Peace Breakers**: 1 Cor- 1:10-13. I Corinthians 3:3 describes the carnal characteristics of a peace breaker. It says, "For ye are yet carnal: for whereas there is among you envying, and strife, and divisions, are ye not carnal, and walk as men?" The word carnal in this verse is the Greek word σαρκικος which means under the control of the animal appetites, governed by mere human nature not by the spirit of God, only connected to the body (senses). The word envying is the Greek word ζήλος which is an envious and contentious rivalry, jealousy, punitive zeal which is fault finding, quick to punish, and desiring to punish. These types of people shatter our peace. The word strife is the Greek word

Ερις which means contention, debaters, argumentative and dissident (Rom.1:29). Then there is the Greek word διχοστασία which means division and divisive. This would be one to create disunion. They are dissentious with a strong tendency to disagree coupled with a difference in sentiment and opinion along with a bad spirit and/or attitude. This should not be because the Bible says this is carnal (1 Corinthians 3:3).

3. **Peace takers**: Luke 22:24. The New Living Translation says, "Then they began to argue among themselves about who would be the greatest." Peace takers are those in which this verse shows as Jesus was making His way to the cross to die for the sins of the world (their sins included), they began to argue and move away from the weightier things like Jesus and His work on the cross. They are arguing over foolishness for the sake of having the attention put on themselves. They are prideful, shallow, and solipsistic at the same time. This group is a "A Trichotomous Mess."

The Bible says in Psalm 34:14, "Depart from evil, and do good; seek peace, and pursue it." Notice here, the Bible commands us in the imperative mood to seek and pursue peace. It is just that important. These are true riches that nothing on earth can provide you with outside of the Prince of Prince – who is Jesus Christ – Our Lord.

Conclusion

I would like to leave us with the significance of quotients which are degrees or amounts of a specified quality or characteristic:

IQ – Intellectual Quotient = Intelligence Quotient

EQ – Emotional Quotient = Emotional Intelligence

SQ – Spiritual Quotient = Intellectual Quotient PLUS Emotional Quotient

Please note the technical definition is the sum of our Intellectual Quotient and Emotional Quotient. Also note, if you could dissect the three quotients in which technically you can't, but if you could, the IQ is more related to the soul and is more knowing and feelings whereby the handling thereof is more spiritually based on what one believes which measures ones EQ or more accurately stated emotional intelligence which determines behavior which is an accurate measurement of one's EQ.

Conclusively... Jesus acquired our salvation pragmatically speaking through proper IQ, EQ and SQ. He knew what to do (that is IQ), he did not allow his emotions to derail, distract, deter, or side-track him (that is EQ), and lastly, He did what the Father said versus what He felt (that is SQ).

WALK WITH THE KING AND BE A BLESSING!

APPENDIX:

DIFFERENT GREEK WORDS DEFINING ANGER

Strong's Greek

ὀργίζω orgízō; fut. orgísō, from orgḗ, wrath. To make angry, provoke. In the NT, only in the mid. / pass. orgízomai, aor. orgísthēn, to be or become angry, provoked (Matt. 18:34; 22:7; Luke 14:21; 15:28; Eph. 4:26; Rev. 11:18). Followed by the dat. (Matt. 5:22); with epí, upon (Rev. 12:17; Sept.: Num. 25:3; 1 Kgs. 11:9; Is. 12:1).

Deriv.: parorgízō, to arouse to wrath, provoke.

Syn.: puróō,to burn up with anger or passion; phruássō,to rage; aphrízō to foam with anger; ōrúomai,to roar; thumóō,to be very angry; exegeírō,to arouse, instigate; choláō,to be melancholy, irritable; aganaktéō,to be indignant; erethízō to provoke; diegeírō,to stir up; paroxúnō,to exasperate, provoke.

Ant.: egkrateúomai, to exercise self-restraint, be temperate; eupsuchéō, to be in good spirits; katastéllō, to appease; hēsucházō, to hold one's peace, be quiet; eirēnopoiéō, to be a peacemaker; sunéchomai, to control oneself

REFERENCES

- Louw-Nida Greek English Lexicon (Dictionary of Biblical Languages with Semantic Domains: Greek (New Testament – Lamb's book)
- Google
- Spirit Controlled Temperaments, Tim Lahaye pg V. of introduction
- Lahaye pg. viii of introduction
- http://interpersonal-compatibility.blogspot.com/2013/12/sanguine-temperament-strengths-and-weaknesses.html
- http://interpersonal-compatibility.blogspot.com/2013/11/choleric-temperament-strengths-weaknesses.html
- http://www.temperamentcounselinginc.com/strengths-and-weaknesses.html
- http://interpersonal-compatibility.blogspot.com/2014/04/phlegmatic-temperament-strengths-and-weaknesses.html
- http://temperaments.fighunter.com/?page=what
- Personality Disorders in Modern Life – Theordore Millon Roger Davis – year 2000- John wiley & Sons – Canada – page 512 -513

---

[i] Louw-Nida Greek English Lexicon (Dictionary of Biblical Languages with Semantic Domains: Greek (New Testament – Lam's book)
[ii] Google
[iii] Spirit Controlled Temperaments, Tim Lahaye pg V. of introduction
[iv]Lahaye pg. viii of introduction
[v] http://interpersonal-compatibility.blogspot.com/2013/12/sanguine-temperament-strengths-and-weaknesses.html
[vi] http://interpersonal-compatibility.blogspot.com/2013/11/choleric-temperament-strengths-weaknesses.html
[vii] http://www.temperamentcounselinginc.com/strengths-and-weaknesses.html
[viii] http://interpersonal-compatibility.blogspot.com/2014/04/phlegmatic-temperament-strengths-and-weaknesses.html
[ix] http://temperaments.fighunter.com/?page=what